A POETESS SOUL WRAPPED IN WORDS

Kajol Chourasia

ISBN 978-93-5559-086-2

Published in India 2021 by Pencil

A brand of
One Point Six Technologies Pvt. Ltd.
123, Building J2, Shram Seva Premises,
Wadala Truck Terminal, Wadala (E)
Mumbai 400037, Maharashtra, INDIA
E connect@thepencilapp.com
W www.thepencilapp.com

Author biography

Kajol Chourasia is an young Chartered Accountant and just entering into the world of corporate career. She is also a Certified Creative Writing Specialist and social media influencer on Instagram. Her unique thoughts and charm mesmerizes her audience. She is a dreamer, and an achiever. She believes in serving humanity and happiness in this world. You may connect with her personally on her Instagram Page- "Heaven_of_quotesnpoem".

Email- Kajalchourasia97@gmail.com

CONTENTS

Acknowledgements

No book can be a reality through the sole efforts of the author. I am hugely indebted to my dear friends for extending their full support.

I thank my family and friends for believing and supporting me. I would also like to extend my gratitude to the institution Henry Harvin from where I pursued my Creative writing course and it gave wings to my writing passion.

I heartily thank my readers to add this book in their reading list and to honour my efforts for writing. I dedicate my passion and success to people in my life and my dear readers.

1. Married to Dream

My heart is clinching my soul inside,

Crying like a new-born-baby just arrived.

My dreams are breathing to its end,

Like a half-dead-body laying somewhere bend.

My time seems to pass by each and every second,

Reducing probability of living life to slend.

I want to get rid of this delusion of being alive,

Where the fact is I'm travelling from the cradle to grave every second.

I want to breath freedom through this god gifted life,

Where all I want is just to get *married to my dreams.*

2. Timeless Love

My heart is as delicate as a flower Rose,

Will you be able to hold it gently?

The way my heart beats for you till infinity,

Will you be able to feel my throbs endlessly?

It's matured for this world but dollish for you,

Will you be able to pamper it with utmost care?

It wants lifetime assurance of you being with me,

Will you be able to give that assurance to me?

And finally, the way I feel you are *timeless*for me,

Will you be also able to make me feel the same perpetually?

Short Phrase 1.

She asked him for a promise not to fall in love ever with her. He promised too, to remain his best friend. Eventually, he fell for her but was afraid to admit it because of the promise he made.

One day he got married and thought of surprising her with this news.

The moment she told him, "stupid, I love you, and I thought you loved me too."

Agony shivered through his heart when he heard those words too late.

3. The Rainbow

Several colours filled the entire sky.

Certainly looked like someone saying 'Hi' before a 'Good-Bye'.

Beautiful flowers felt jealousy over the joy.

Eye-popping is the hue endearing sky like some toy.

The horde of people gathered evidencing the view.

Wow! That's a rainbow with seven incredible hues.

Many bumped into each other staring towards the azure sky.

Increased is the pleasure of seeing above clouds glorified.

Beautiful is the colour of life like those rainbows in the sky.

Pain is a colour too with a lesson to live by.

Happiness is a moment to let life feel dignified.

Forget all worries and live before you get disqualified.

Ending my verses with this much only to intensify

Remember the lesson above and never let it untie.

A rainbow is an object but happiness is mystify.

Let's promise to live utmost before we die.

4. You & I

Hey listen,

What?

I want to be

with you forever.

But you wanted me to set you

free?

I was stupid.

Yes, you are!

Just shut up!

You were stupid

to let me go.

Yes I'm, b'cos I can do

anything just to see you happy.

Pagal.

I'm sorry...

And they embraced each other tightly.....

Short Phrase 2.

She wore heavy makeup to look pretty and entered the club. People swaying on the floor kept staring at her as if she is an alien. She disregarded them all and kept dancing madly. A girl swaying nearby sneered, "You should first learn how to put on makeup before trying to be the center of attraction." Others too laughed at her.

After a while, when people saw her serving others in a waitress outfit, the sight was heartbreaking. She was an acid attack survivor celebrating her 25th birthday alone just before the duty.

5. The Life

Grudges about the past.

The concern of the future.

The predicament of the present.

Life changed a lot.

Days passed like some drops in the sea.

Months hopped by like some flowing river.

Years flew by like some broken Dam.

The time flew without apprising life.

Leaving behind some known faces.

Holding inside some etched pains.

Forgiving heart for some misfortunes.

The life turned out callous.

The irony of losing everything.

The fear of reaching nowhere.

The guilt of missing true self.

Life took a major U-turn.

6. The Lost

Walking down the lane,

Wandering around in the plane.

Searching my lost soul,

With some grudges & wounds.

Protesting storm emerging inside,

Letting the low sweep anger behind.

Accepting flaws with a courageous mind,

Though life is a road yet to unwind.

Eyelids flashing some faces every time

Often their true colour, with a fake smile.

Though I know it's futile to remind,

Oh yes, there is a lesson behind.

I'll walk further now it's only nine,

My soul needs some further time.

To bounce back It's ok to feel lost sometimes,

B'cos life is chess you'll be checkmate anytime.

Short Phrase 3.

He compiled all loose leaf written by her and got it published. Within the next few years, she emerged as a renowned author.

One day, she dedicated her success to him in an award function. When she announced his name on the stage everyone was shocked seeing him.

He was blind thirty-one years old man who lost his sight in an accident while trying to save her from committing suicide.

7. Unstoppable

They said, she can't.

She said, she will.

They said, she lacks resources.

She believed, she had her.

They said, she is weak.

She proved, she is ambitious.

They said, she is ordinary.

She illustrated, she is rare.

They said, she is hopeless.

She perceived, she is optimistic.

They said, she is overconfident.

She showed, she is determined.

They said, she will fall.

She knew, she will emerge.

They said, she will give up.

Yet, she is unstoppable.

8. The Charismatic She

Tap-Tap, Tap-Tap

The sound grabbed everyones attention,

When entered she.

Her Pleasant smile, confident eye

Vibrant personality, Elegant look

Wow! She is marvelous.

Her worthy views, focused mind

Gentle tone, snapping to gain attention

OMG! She is lady boss.

Her leadership traits, eye opener talk,

A beautiful soul with generous voice.

Aah! She inspires me.

Short Phrase 4.

She kept crying, pleading before him not to leave her but he walked off without giving a second thought.

After 5 years, A girl entered lavishly with her husband in a 5 star hotel. All the staff members obeyed her as if she is the queen. In the same hotel he was having dinner with his wife, the view was unbelievable to him. On enquiring he came to know she was the owner of this hotel.

After finishing his dinner when he peeped at the table sitting she, his heart skipped a beat. She was the same girl he broke up 5 years back.

9. The wait

From the moment

Getting announcement notification

Till my fate flashed on the screen

The wait was tough.

Heartbeats fluctuating every now & then

Mind speculating the outcome-

The happiness of success

The sorrow of failure.

Time spoke to me

Like some invisible soul.

Feeling disinterested in doing chores

Informing everyone about its arrival.

Sleepless night with unwelcome thoughts

Waking up early subtracting one

Oh my God!

The result is OUT

With the word 'PASS' on its face.

Finally, the wait was worth

All sleepless nights.

10. Limitless

It has no name,

No colour

Nor physical appearance

But still, it exists.

Then,

What is it called?

Maybe,

It's Love?

But why?

B'cos,

It's an intense feeling

Of deep affection.

Is it unconditional?

Yes!

It should be

But it's not always.

Is there any form of it?

No!

It has no form

But it can be in any form.

Is it person-specific?

Sometimes,

But not limited to the person only

It can be anything.

Do I need to pay something in return?

Yes!

Nothing is free

Love demands love in consideration.

Does it has any limit?

No!

It's limitless

Although it's rare.

Short Phrase 5

Their marriage was merely an agreement to live together with no hope of love. Everyone in the family was so happy without knowing the inside story.

However, After few years the scene was different.

When she was on her death bed, she grieved and apologized to him for the revenge she was taking for marrying her against her wish.

Lamentably, burning in the fire of revenge ultimately led to the death.

11. Morning Bliss

The Cloudy Ice buried the mountains beneath its bosom.

May be again it's time to make this world look awesome.

Sun saying good-bye to moon taking its turn to light this world.

One Missing this wonderful view should definitely be a nerd.

Birds started chirping leaving their nest in search of food.

Filling the azure sky like a printed blanket to look good.

Owl started loosing its eyesight once again for rest of the day.

Evidencing the transition from colorful to colorless for whole day.

Plants giving birth to new baby-flower each day.

Honeybees wandering around them to extract honey & play.

Probably again it is time for human-wanderers to leave their nest.

Finding the purpose of life each day is something that should be the best.

12. Turning The Page

My crawling words cried on the shoulder of my page like some insane.

My bleeding ink pleaded me to turn the page once again.

Making me sense palpable happiness like snow in the rain.

Forbidding my veins from recalling the grief once again.

Uttering the words of grief flowing like blood in my veins.

Begging me to live the life with love & zeal once again.

All the time requesting me to bury that unbearable pain,

And to fill my life with beautiful adventure once again.

Forgiving those people shattering me like a drop on the dusty land,

Hey! Why not to *turn the page*and live this life once again.

Short Phrase 6.

He said, 'You are very beautiful.'

She replied, 'appreciate my heart if you want me to say you 'Thank You', because that's what I have really worked on.'

13. Lets Start Fresh

I want to raise high

Like a Mountain

And roar like a Lioness.

Why to cry recalling the Past

And destroying the Future,

By ruining the Present.

All I just wanna say is-

Why not to forget everything

And lets start Fresh.

14. A Warm Hug

Bumping into you was a coincidence.

But Meeting you was my fate.

Talking to you was my choice.

But falling in love with you was natural.

Dating you was my passion.

But teasing you was my fun.

Walking with you was my journey.

But marrying you was my dream.

Playing with your hair was my hobby.

But staring your eyes was my sedative.

Caressing your skin was my ritual.

But kissing your lips was my destiny.

Everytime all I needed when I saw you,

Was just 'you' and 'a warm hug'.

Short Phrase 7.

They walked together but weren't together.

Then why did they walk together?

They were returning from the court after divorce.

15. Wheel of Fortune

She germinated in this world,

Like an unwanted ivy covering the castle.

She screamed as loud as a firecracker for a cradle,

But settled in despair with tears in the stony earth.

She wanted to elevate like Mount Everest.

But ended up being the victim of circumstances.

She craved for approval of her existence in this world.

While burying down grudges of freedom inside her heart.

Then one fine day accidentally she met a man of her words

Who turned her world like an hourglass upside-down.

Creator of fate turned the wheel of fortune this time

Finally! By all means, destiny found her on time.

16. A Speaking Tree

I stand rooted in all the season,
Fearlessly, without any selfish reason.

I invite travellers to take some rest,
Have some sleep then move for next.

I dance madly with the gentle wind.
Singing freely with a rustling sound.

Sometimes, It's a curse to feel paralysed,
But thanks to God, I'm blessed with farsight.

I fight with the storm like a Warrior.
Tirelessly I win, but sometimes I surrender.

Short Phrase 8.

He said, “Beauty with brain is a rare combination.”

She replied, “And that rare combination is sitting in front of you.”

He blinked his eye embracing her beauty...

17. A Revolutionized heart

Carrying a devastated heart,

Stomping in an anonymous park

Lost in her own thoughts

Holding strings of memories

She traveled her past.

Forgiving few dodger faces

Forgetting few heart-wrenching setbacks

Dauntlessly, she moved on.

Burying inside the grudges of past

This time with a stronger heart

Full of determination

And a fire to spark.

Heroically, she found a better self

Revolutionized with a broken heart.

18. Forever Love

I want to be your evergreen

Will you be my blossom?

I want to fill your life with rainbows

Will you add some colours to mine too?

I want to reach glorious heights with you

Will you walk by my side too?

I want to damp your soul with fragrance

Will you add some fragrance to mine too?

I want to make your life heavenly beautiful

Will you make my life worth living too?

I want to be your forever love

Will you be mine too?

Short Phrase 9.

He rejected her, she accepted the fact.

Then after a few years, she rejected everyone.

Why?

To take revenge?

No!

Her upgraded version was difficult to beat...

19. You Complete Me

When you look at me

With your twinkling eyes.

You complete me...

When you clasp your Palm with mine,

Assuring me you are mine forever.

You complete me...

When you hug me tight with all your heart,

Adoring my presence in your life.

You complete me...

When you caress my hair smoothly,

With your slender fingers.

You complete me...

When your lips gently press mine,

Taking my heart on to a rollercoaster ride.

You complete me...

Yes.....!

Whenever you are with me as my reflection,

You truly complete me!

20. When She Got Her Wings

When she got her wings,

She flew.

The crowd kept staring at her,

Thinking she must be an angel.

Winds bedeck her wings,

Sun gifted its shine to her,

Clouds welcomed her,

Highness adored her.

Certainly,

It looked like,

She absorbed this cosmos.

Finally,

After years of hard work,

God returned her sights,

Her strong will compelled him.

She defeated the world twice.

Once,

When she got her sights.

Secondly,

When her Dad said proudly-

Welcome my princess

'IAS officer Janhavi'.

Short Phrase 10.

She traveled the world fearlessly and created the world record at the age of nine.

"Whee! I'm an achiever," She woke up in excitement.

To the world it was just a dream but the glee on her face was worth million views.

21. The Baggage

The baggage he carried

Was invisible.

He carried it daily,

Without taking a pause,

And without taking rest,

He carried it for so long.

With the hope,

One day he will be relieved from this.

Too much stuffy,

Too much bulky,

Yet, he didn't say a word.

She could feel his pain,

But she was helpless.

She tried sharing his baggage,

But soon slumped.

He consoled her.

And moved on.

Then,

One day painfully,

He collapsed while carrying bricks on his head.

And left this world forever,

Free from all the baggage,

Leaving behind

His crippled destitute wife,

And three helpless children.

22. The Nightmare

She was shuddering,

Gripping her pillow tight,

Gazing here and there, everywhere.

Spying every corner of the room.

Staring towards the dark Sky,

Peeking for some hell hound.

The mirror reflected her zombie expression.

Messed hair, furious sight,

Chewing lips, clutched knife.

Surely,

Lifetime imprisonment is the only prophecy.

Water splashed...

Get up stupid!

It's your SSC result date,

Samaira soared taking a sigh of relief.

Thank God! I didn’t kill anyone!

She said quizzically.

Short Phrase 11.

.

He wrote his heart out every day with a hope that one day she will read and realise what he was going through all this while.

Finally One day, she opened her FB account but there was nothing from him. “Alas! Perhaps, he forgot me,” She groaned. Her heart wreathed in agony.

Although she recovered from paralyses after two years, but the suffering was not over...

Tragically, still, he feels she was unfaithful to him.

23. His Victorious Ride

The sky roared like Lion in a dense forest.

Clouds travelled miles bucket full of water.

A bolt of lightning touched the feet of the earth like fire in a meadow.

He toddled straight like a Gun man full of arms.

Kept crawling until he reached the deadly end.

The cosmos admired his victorious giggles.

Auch! I'm stuck in between these flower pots.

The rain started drizzling full of thunderstorms.

She arrived in vein clutched him tight.

Oh, my dear baby!

How could I be so careless to leave you alone like this?

24. The Ocean of Thoughts

I kept starring at the sky,

Thinking one day this universe will absorb me too.

Aah! I feel disheartened.

This thought made me imagine my cremation too.

Every day millions of lives are buried under the ground.

One day I will be buried too.

The ocean of thoughts kept rippling in my mind.

I pinched myself and came back to my senses.

Instantly I promised my little self to give a purpose to this life.

Saying, Dear! You've got only one life.

Live it like a queen who conquered this world.

Give others a reason to remember you once you're gone.

Your departure will leave tears in millions of eyes.

And you will be a twinkling star in the sky forever thereafter!

Abruptly, I smiled and walked down the rooftop of my house.

Short Phrase 12.

He said- Let's walk together, a little more we might end up being together forever.

She replied- “Forever doesn’t exist”, and walked off.

He realized even true love doesn’t exist.

25. Stranger

Hey Stranger,

Will you walk by my side?

And hold my hands tight?

Hey Stranger,

Will you accept me with all my flaws?

And still, love me without any clause?

Hey Stranger,

Will you promise me you are mine?

And let me be your forever sun-shine?

Hey Stranger,

Will you help me to find my real self?

And achieve great success without anyone's help?

Hey Stranger,

Will you love me forever like anything else?

And fill my heart with your love like rose petals?

26. The Wait...

In the darkroom amongst the dead people

She hunched in a corner like a zombie.

Clenching the mobile phone in her delicate hands.

Where her sight traveled along with the clock.

Waiting for something unexpected to occur.

Perhaps It was happening for the first time

Since she fought for her right.

Marrying a stranger was a quest.

Her heartbeats sprinted faster than a marathon.

Fear and tear loaded like water in the jar.

Awwww! The face of the clock struck midnight.

A message flashed on her mobile screen.

'HAPPY BIRTHDAY, beta!'

Tears of joy rolled making their way through her sunken cheeks.

Ouch! Hurting parents was never that easy.

27. The Clouds and Me

A white sheet embracing the cosmos

Limitlessly.

Painting the clouds neatly

With soft cotton balls.

Roving consistently from one end to another

Fascinating me to keep moving too.

The blazing sun playing hide & seek

Every now and then.

Causing the climate change

Like timer set by someone in heaven.

My sights evidencing supreme view

Without blinking even for a second.

Abruptly, some codes passed through my veins

Heavenly God has beautifully painted me too.

www.ingramcontent.com/pod-product-compliance
Lightning Source LLC
LaVergne TN
LVHW050421160726
843469LV00041B/1187

* 9 7 8 9 3 5 5 5 9 0 8 6 2 *